$100

8

PENGUIN

MW00681731

cocktail
bible

cocktail
bible

contents

introduction

Cocktails never seem to go out of fashion. All that seems to vary is the range of base ingredients used and the number of recipes available. And, of course, the way cocktails are presented – with extravagant garnishes one decade and minimalist elegance the next.

You don't need a bar full of bottles to make an impressive array of cocktails: one or two spirits, liqueurs and aperitifs are enough to let you have lots of fun experimenting. In the end, cocktails are about style, flair and presentation, so do invest in a gleaming cocktail shaker and some stylish glasses, and serve your drinks with a flourish.

setting up

Most of the equipment you need for making cocktails you're likely to already have in your kitchen. These include a large **jug** (preferably with a curved lip to stop ice tipping into serving glasses), small **bowls** (handy for holding lemon and lime slices, cherries, olives and the like), **teaspoons** and **tablespoons** (for measuring), a **cutting board** (for preparing garnishes), a **grater** (for grating fresh nutmeg and chocolate for garnishes), a **paring knife** (essential for slicing, cutting and peeling fruit) and a **citrus zester** (to produce fine peel for a garnish or 'twist').

Use a small **juice squeezer** when you need fresh lemon, lime, orange and grapefruit juices; a **citrus reamer** is efficient for small quantities of juice. A **juice extractor** is useful (if noisy) if you plan on making lots of fresh, fruity cocktails.

A **blender** is excellent for making frothy cocktails. Unless it is a *very* powerful model, only use crushed ice (or crack the cubes before putting them in the blender).

The most versatile **bottle opener and corkscrew** is the 'bartender's friend', which can peel the wrapping from the neck of the bottle, pull a cork and open a can. But there are myriad varieties.

bar equipment

There are a few more specialised tools that are invaluable for mixing cocktails.

A classic **cocktail shaker** is usually made of metal (often stainless steel or silver), incorporates a strainer and has a tight-fitting lid. A Boston shaker has a metal base and a glass top (easier to see the ingredients) but no strainer. If your shaker doesn't have an inbuilt **strainer,** you will need a separate one: the distinctive 'Hawthorn strainer', with a wire spring encircling the rim, is favoured by most bartenders.

A lidded **ice-bucket** will help stop the ice from melting too quickly. **Ice-tongs** are handy for picking up ice (without extra water) and for handling fruit garnishes. An **ice-scoop** is great for ladling ice in larger quantities.

A heavy hand with the alcohol does not make the best cocktails – balancing the flavours is important. A double-ended **measure** (15 ml and 30 ml) is practical: if you don't have a measure, note that 1 teaspoon = 5 ml and 1 tablespoon = 20 ml in Australia (15 ml in the UK and US). Serious mixologists might consider having a **measuring pourer** (or jigger) that fits on the top of a spirit bottle that you use often.

Specialist extras include a **muddler**, a long-handled implement with a flattened end, used for mashing fruit, herbs, spices or sugar. (You can use the handle of a wooden spoon instead.) For stirring and other uses, it's handy to have a long-handled **bar spoon** with a twisted handle (so it won't slip). You may also want to keep a supply of **swizzle sticks**, colourful **straws**, and **toothpicks.**

stocking the bar

How well you stock the bar depends on how you intend to use it, how often, for how many, and what type of drinks you plan on serving. As a rule of thumb, think quality instead of quantity and extend your bar as you extend your repertoire. Invest in half-size bottles if you are just setting up but want variety.

Start with your **spirits** – a good dry gin, a clear vodka, some brandy and a reasonable-quality rum (either white or light, or both) and possibly tequila. You may have a favourite whiskey, or prefer Scotch whisky. Bourbon is needed for mint juleps, and cachaça (a Brazilian spirit) for the ever-so-fashionable caipirinha cocktails.

For **liqueurs**, triple sec (basically an orange-flavoured liqueur) is essential, with Cointreau and Grand Marnier being more luxurious versions if your budget stretches to them. Blackcurrant-flavoured crème de cassis is a sophisticated addition to sparkling wine. Kahlua and Frangelico are popular for creamy cocktails, while the coconut-rum Malibu is in demand amongst many younger drinkers.

You will need one or two **aperitifs** if you are planning to make iconic cocktails. Dry vermouth is essential for a Martini, while sweet vermouth and the slightly bitter Italian aperitif Campari make the jewel-like red Negroni and a range of other classics.

And, of course, any well-stocked bar should always have **sparkling** white wine or champagne on hand.

As to more basic ingredients, **bitters** add distinctive flavour to cocktails, and Angostura bitters should definitely be your first choice. Of the flavoured syrups **grenadine**, a pomegranate syrup, is widely used. For soft-drink **mixers**, soda water, lemonade and cola are probably the minimum, and you might add dry ginger ale.

For **juices,** think lemon and lime juice, best squeezed fresh. Orange juice and cranberry juice are versatile, and mango, pineapple, and tomato juice are other possibilities.

Sugar syrup is called for in some drinks. To make your own, heat 1 cup of water with 1 cup of castor sugar. Bring to boil, and then simmer without stirring for about 5 minutes, until the sugar is completely dissolved. Cool, and store in a covered bottle in the refrigerator. It is also possible to buy a ready-made sweet syrup called **gomme**. If you use sugar, is used it should be superfine castor sugar.

For creamy cocktails, **cream** and **milk** might be called for. **Coconut cream** is used to make Piña Colada.

Assorted extras might include castor sugar and salt for frosting glasses (see page 12), pepper and Worcestershire sauce or Tabasco for a zesty Bloody Mary. And, of course, it's essential to have on hand an assortment of garnishes (see page 11).

garnishes

When garnishing, remember – less is more. A simple olive in a Martini, one perfect strawberry for a Champagne Cocktail, or a sliver of fresh peel in a Daiquiri is ample. Having said that, some drinks lend themselves to a little extravagance – a sugar-frosted rim, a pineapple spear and fresh cherries, or even straws, swizzle stick and – why not? – sometimes even a cocktail umbrella.

Classic additions Maraschino cherries, green olives (in brine, preferably unstuffed).

Fruits Fresh lemons, limes and oranges are imperative, while strawberries, pineapple and melon are among the many possible fruity garnishes.

Herbs Basil and mint for starters – use the freshest, softest, baby leaves.

Toppings Chocolate – grated, or use a peeler to make long curls. Others include ground cinnamon, dusted on with a light hand; fresh coconut grated into strips; and freshly grated nutmeg.

to frost a glass

The distinctive profile of the traditional cocktail glass is best suited to this technique, which will give your drinks a professional but fun edge.

Hold the glass by the stem and dip the rim into lightly beaten egg white, juice (such as lemon, lime, cranberry), syrup (such as grenadine), or even a liqueur (such as Frangelico). Put castor sugar into a flat dish, press the rim of the glass into the sugar and turn the glass slowly. When the rim is coated, turn the glass upright and tap lightly to remove any excess.

To salt-frost, use lemon or lime juice and salt.

preparing fruit

Always use the best-quality fruit and make sure it is absolutely fresh and clean. Fruit (peel left on) can be cut in slices, rings, quarters or halves. Cut pineapple into small triangles or long spears.

To make a **twist,** use a paring knife to cut a small strip of citrus zest (no bitter pith), then twist this over the drink to release the fragrant oils. The twist is often dropped or floated in the glass for added flavour and aroma. For a **spiral**, use a paring knife to cut a strip of peel about 5 mm wide and 10–15 cm long, then curl it by hand. (If making spirals ahead of time, twist around a pencil or spoon handle.)

For a **knot,** use a peeler to cut a long strip of peel, tie gently into a knot and then drop into the drink.

strawberry on the side

If mounting a strawberry on the rim of the glass, leave the leaves on, then cut the fruit almost in half. To fan it, make several slits in the fruit.

melon balls

Use a melon-baller to shape the fruit, then spear each ball on a toothpick.

ice

You need ice, ice and then a little more ice. Keep in mind that large ice cubes melt more slowly (so keeping a drink cold without diluting it too much). You can also set slivers of citrus fruit, mint leaves or berries in ice cubes to serve, or you can have ice cubes shaped as stars or diamonds.

If you don't have crushed ice, wrap cubes in a clean tea towel and break them up using a kitchen mallet or rolling pin.

how to make the perfect cocktail

For the cocktail connoisseur, preparing cocktails is both an art and a craft. There are rules for many of the classics – stirred not shaken, shaken not rocked to sleep – and there are techniques to master. But cocktails are inherently frivolous, so a little practice, a little tasting and a little tinkering will ensure drinks perfectly tailored to your own style. Chin chin!

how to shake

Half-fill the bottom of a cocktail shaker or Boston shaker with ice cubes. Add spirits, liqueurs and mixers (don't over-fill the shaker), put the lid on tightly and shake for about 10 to 20 seconds (too much shaking can dilute the drink). Then carefully undo the lid and strain the drink into a clean serving glass.

how many drinks per bottle?

The average shot of alcohol (spirits or liqueur) used for cocktail-making is 45 ml. (Thus 1 x 750 ml bottle = approximately 16 drinks.) In a bar or hotel, however, 30 ml is a standard shot.

how many cocktails

If you are having a cocktail party, it is advisable to limit the variety of cocktails (to ensure you don't run out of ingredients).

Allow around 3–4 cocktails per person over 2 hours, though this does depend on the strength of the cocktails (they are meant to be sipped at a very leisurely pace).

For 8–15 guests, offer 2–3 varieties of cocktail.

For 15–25 guests, offer 3–4 varieties of cocktail.

For 25–50 guests, offer 4 varieties of cocktail.

tips

- Buy good-quality alcohol and mixers.
- Store gin and vodka in the freezer for ice-cold aperitifs.
- Clean, polish and chill your drinking glasses. Handle them by the stem to keep the glass clean and cool.
- Measure your ingredients to get the balance right.
- Use fresh fruit whenever possible, but especially for lemon, lime and orange juices.

- Always have plenty of fresh, clean ice on hand.
- Serve generous amounts of food with your cocktails.
- Include some stylish non-alcoholic 'mocktails' in your repertoire.

note

Most cocktails contain more than one shot of alcohol and often a combination of liquors, which means they are potent and often the equivalent of more than one 'normal' drink. So drink responsibly, and if you drink, don't drive.

glasses

When serving cocktails, remember that the better it looks, the better it will taste. For iconic cocktails (a Martini, a Manhattan) thin-lipped, transparent glasses that 'ping' when flicked are perfect. But cocktails are also fun, so choose glasses to reflect your own style – funky and coloured, retro classics or sleek and modern – and make sure they gleam.

Wash glasses well, rinse and wipe, then polish with a lint-free cloth.

Glasses should be chilled for most cocktails (the exception might be a warming cognac-based concoction). To chill glasses, place in the refrigerator or freezer, or swish some ice cubes in the glass, then dry and polish.

Some of the most popular glass shapes are shown on the following page. Each recipe in this book indicates the type of glass traditionally used, but as you'll see from the photographs you can feel free to vary these. And remember – a stemmed glass will help keep a drink cold, as it protects the bowl of the glass from the warmth of your hand.

brandy balloon or goblet

Holds 200–300 ml. A generous size and shape, ideal for sophisticated brandy-based cocktails or frothy, heavily garnished concoctions.

champagne flute

About 150 ml. A tall, elegant shape, perfect for sparkling drinks that need to hold their bubbles.

champagne saucer or coupe

About 150 ml. Rarely used these days for fine champagne or sparkling wines (the bubbles are quickly lost) but a distinctive shape and an excellent alternative to a traditional cocktail glass.

cocktail or martini

About 90 ml. The classic shape for a classic cocktail such as a Martini or a Manhattan. Larger sizes (up to 300 ml) are available for more exotic drinks that include various liqueurs and juices as well, allowing room for garnishes.

highball

About 200–300 ml. A tall, straight-sided glass designed for refreshing long drinks, and often suitable for non-alcoholic drinks. The tallest versions are sometimes called a Collins, after the cocktail of the same name.

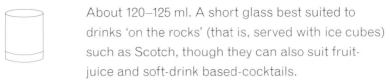

old-fashioned

About 120–125 ml. A short glass best suited to drinks 'on the rocks' (that is, served with ice cubes) such as Scotch, though they can also suit fruit-juice and soft-drink based-cocktails.

pilsener

About 210–300 ml. A tall, elegant glass, often V-shaped, suitable for beer, pilsener, or drinks mixed with sparkling wine.

shot glass

About 30–60 ml. Very short, thick glass suitable for a shot of alcohol; the preferred glass for 'shooters'.

wine glass

About 150–200 ml. A red wine glass tends to have a larger bowl and hold more than a white wine glass. Shapes and sizes vary enormously. The stem is ideal because it means the hand does not touch the bowl of the glass, so the contents stay cold.

bourbon

algonquin

60 ml bourbon or rye whiskey
30 ml dry vermouth
30 ml pineapple juice

Shake ingredients well with ice,
then strain into a short glass
and serve on the rocks.

suggested glass: old-fashioned

A classic whiskey cocktail in honour of the legendary Algonquin
Hotel, renowned as a haunt for New York's cocktail-drinking literati
in the early 20th century, including famous writer, poet and satirist
Dorothy Parker.

frisco sour

30 ml bourbon
30 ml Bénédictine
7 ml lemon juice
7 ml lime juice
lemon and lime slices
for garnish

Shake all the ingredients well with ice, then strain into a well-chilled wine glass. Twist the lemon and lime slices together on a toothpick and balance on the rim of the glass.

suggested glass: wine glass

highball

45 ml bourbon
dry ginger ale or soda water
lemon peel for a twist

Put a generous quantity of ice cubes in a highball glass, then add the bourbon. Top with dry ginger or soda water. Twist the lemon, drop it in and serve.

suggested glass: highball

mint julep

4–5 fresh mint leaves
1 teaspoon castor sugar
60 ml bourbon
soda water
sprig of mint for garnish

Use a muddler or wooden spoon to crush the mint leaves with the sugar in a highball glass. Pour in bourbon and stir until sugar is dissolved. Add some ice cubes, top with soda water and garnish with a sprig of fresh mint.

suggested glass: highball

brandy

american beauty

20 ml brandy
20 ml dry vermouth
7 ml white crème de menthe
20 ml orange juice
dash of grenadine
30 ml port

Shake all the ingredients, except the port, with ice. Strain into a glass, then slowly pour the port on top.

suggested glass: old-fashioned or wine glass

b & b

30 ml brandy (or cognac for a special occasion)

30 ml Bénédictine

Pour the brandy and Bénédictine slowly into a warmed brandy balloon. Stir gently and serve.

suggested glass: brandy balloon

between the sheets

30 ml brandy
30 ml light rum
30 ml Cointreau
15 ml lemon juice
lemon peel for garnish

Shake all ingredients well with ice. Strain into a champagne saucer or cocktail glass and garnish with a sliver of lemon peel.

suggested glass: champagne saucer or cocktail glass

brandy alexander

60 ml brandy
30 ml crème de cacao
30 ml heavy pouring cream
freshly grated nutmeg
for garnish

Shake the ingredients well with ice, then strain into a chilled cocktail glass. Sprinkle nutmeg on top.

suggested glass: cocktail glass

brandy crusta

30 ml orange juice
30 ml brandy
30 ml orange curaçao
spiral of orange peel
for garnish

Dip the rim of a cocktail glass into orange juice and then sugar-frost it (see page 12). Shake all the ingredients well with ice. Strain into the prepared glass and drape the spiral of peel on the rim of the glass.

suggested glass: cocktail glass

brandy flip

45 ml brandy
1 small egg
1 teaspoon castor sugar
grated nutmeg for garnish

Shake all ingredients with ice, or blend in a blender, and strain into a wine glass. Dust with nutmeg.

suggested glass: wine glass

If a cocktail has an egg in it, break the egg into a separate dish first to make sure it is fresh – and so that you don't waste any alcohol.

caipirinha

1 small lime, cut into
8 wedges
2 teaspoons castor sugar
60 ml cachaça

Muddle the lime wedges and
sugar in a cocktail shaker.
Add ice cubes and cachaça,
shake well and then pour into
glass (the wedges are served
in the glass).

suggested glass: old-fashioned

This fashionable cocktail, pronounced 'kie-pur-REEN-yah',
uses a potent Brazilian spirit made from sugarcane.
For a Cherry Caipirinha add a dash of crème de cassis.
A Caipirissima uses white rum instead of cachaça.

cherry blossom

15 ml cherry brandy
45 ml brandy
few drops curaçao
few drops grenadine
15 ml lemon juice

Sugar-frost a chilled cocktail glass using the cherry brandy (see page 12). Combine all ingredients with ice, shake well, then strain into prepared glass.

suggested glass: cocktail glass

maxim's

15 ml brandy
15 ml Cointreau
1 teaspoon raspberry liqueur
15 ml orange juice
75 ml champagne or
sparkling wine
orange slice for garnish

Half-fill mixing glass with ice.
Pour in brandy, Cointreau,
raspberry liqueur and orange
juice. Stir and then pour into
a champagne saucer. Top with
champagne. Twist the orange
slice and place on the rim.

suggested glass: champagne
saucer

pisco sour

60 ml pisco
45 ml lemon or lime juice
1 teaspoon castor sugar
dash of Angostura bitters
(optional)

Combine all ingredients in
a shaker with ice and shake
well. Strain into a chilled
cocktail glass.

suggested glass: cocktail glass

Pisco is a type of clear brandy made from muscat grapes,
produced in Chile and Peru. Both countries claim the Pisco Sour
as their national drink. Some versions have egg white,
which creates a frothy top.

sidecar

60 ml brandy or cognac
7 ml Cointreau
7 ml lemon juice
spiral of lemon peel
for garnish

Shake ingredients well with ice and strain into a cocktail glass. Drop the spiral of lemon peel in the drink.

suggested glass: cocktail glass

gin

alaska

60 ml London dry gin
15 ml Yellow Chartreuse
lemon peel for a twist
spiral of lemon peel for
garnish

Pour gin and Chartreuse into mixing glass or jug with ice, and stir. Then strain into a cocktail glass and add a twist of lemon, and some shaved ice if you like. Drape the spiral of lemon peel over the rim or across the top of the glass.

suggested glass: cocktail glass

blue bayou

30 ml gin
15 ml Galliano
15 ml dry vermouth
15 ml blue curaçao
lemonade
slice of lemon and a cherry
for garnish

Combine all ingredients, except lemonade, with ice and shake well. Strain into a tall glass, add ice cubes and ice-cold lemonade. Garnish with lemon slice and cherry, and serve with a straw for slow sipping.

suggested glass: highball

campari crush

30 ml gin
15 ml Campari
ruby grapefruit juice
lime wedge for garnish

Fill a tall glass with ice. Pour in gin and Campari, then top with grapefruit juice. Squeeze a little lime juice into the drink, then drop in the lime wedge and serve.

suggested glass: highball

gibson

60 ml gin (or vodka)
a few dashes dry vermouth
2–3 cocktail onions

Stir the gin with ice cubes in a mixing glass then strain into a chilled cocktail glass. Skewer 2–3 cocktail onions and place in the glass.

suggested glass: cocktail glass

This is really a Dry Martini with cocktail onions instead of an olive or a twist. Cocktail connoisseurs are so specific about their ingredients that a new garnish warrants a new name.

gimlet

45 ml gin
10 ml lime cordial
spiral of lime peel for garnish

Shake the gin and cordial well with ice. Strain into a cocktail glass, add an ice cube or two, and drop the lime peel into the drink.

suggested glass: cocktail glass

Some drinkers enjoy a splash of soda in this classic drink, and some recent versions substitute vodka for gin.

gin fizz

60 ml gin
30 ml lemon juice
15 ml lime juice
1 tablespoon castor sugar
soda water

Shake the gin, fruit juices and sugar with ice until well mixed, then strain into a highball glass. Add soda water and stir to make it fizz. Serve immediately.

suggested glass: highball

There is a whole category of cocktails known as 'fizzes', using a range of spirits. For a refreshing Elderflower Fizz add 15 ml elderflower cordial in place of lime juice.

green dragon

60 ml gin
30 ml crème de menthe
15 ml Jägermeister
15 ml lime juice
a few dashes orange bitters

Combine ingredients with ice and shake well. Strain into a chilled cocktail glass.

suggested glass: cocktail glass

martini (classic dry)

45 ml gin
5 ml vermouth (see note below)
lemon peel for a twist
olive (optional)

Stir the gin and vermouth with ice cubes in a mixing glass until just chilled. Quickly strain into a chilled cocktail glass, twist the peel over the cocktail (but don't add the peel to the glass) and add an olive (if you must).

suggested glass: cocktail glass

This is the quintessential cocktail – James Bond's preferred tipple ('shaken not stirred'), the stuff of myth and legend. It can never be too cold or too dry. The dryness hinges on the amount of vermouth: aficionados claim the less the better, in some cases no more than wafting the vermouth bottle across the cocktail glass. Winston Churchill reputedly glanced at the vermouth bottle as he poured the gin. For a Sweet Martini use sweet vermouth instead of dry. For a Perfect Martini use sweet and dry vermouth (total of 5 ml).

monkey gland

45 ml gin
5 ml Pernod
45 ml orange juice
a few drops of grenadine
slice of orange peel for
garnish (optional)

Shake ingredients briefly with
ice, then strain into a chilled
cocktail glass and serve.

suggested glass: cocktail glass

This is a classic cocktail with an impressive pedigree,
first mentioned in the 1930 classic *Savoy Cocktail Book* by
Harry Craddock, the so-called 'master of the swizzle stick'.

pink gin

several dashes
Angostura bitters

45 ml Plymouth gin (or London
dry gin, if you prefer)

iced water (optional)

Pour the bitters into a short glass, roll it around to coat the sides, and then tip out any excess. Pour in the gin, add a little ice or a splash of iced water.

suggested glass: old-fashioned

This cocktail was famed throughout the old British Empire for its supposed medicinal properties (owing to the bitters), and was traditionally consumed tepid, or at room temperature. It is also known as Gin and Bitters. The classic Gin and Tonic (G&T) was also considered a preventative for malaria as the tonic water contained quinine.

pink pussycat

60 ml gin
pineapple juice
dash of grenadine
pineapple spear for garnish

Fill a glass two-thirds with ice cubes. Pour in gin, top up with pineapple juice and add a dash of grenadine. Stir gently, then add pineapple spear for garnish.

suggested glass: highball

singapore sling

45 ml gin
10 ml cherry brandy
15 ml lemon juice
1 teaspoon castor sugar
soda water
slice of lemon for garnish

Shake gin, brandy, juice and sugar well with ice. Strain into a tall glass, add an ice cube and top with soda water. Twist the lemon slice, skewer with a toothpick and then balance on the glass.

suggested glass: highball

This is sometimes known as The Sling.
For a Gin Sling, omit the cherry brandy.

tom collins

60 ml gin
45 ml lemon juice
7 ml sugar syrup
soda water
lemon peel for a twist

Stir gin, juice and sugar syrup in a very tall glass. Add plenty of ice cubes and soda, and a twist of lemon.

suggested glass: highball

A Pierre Collins uses cognac instead of gin.
A Sandy Collins uses Scotch whisky.
A Pedro Collins uses rum.

liqueurs & aperitifs

alabama slammer

15 ml Southern Comfort
15 ml sloe gin
10 ml amaretto
30 ml pineapple juice

Shake ingredients with ice.
Strain into a chilled glass.

suggested glass: old-fashioned

There are numerous recipes for an Alabama Slammer.
Some have much more fruit juice and are served in a long glass,
while others contain just a dash of juice and are served in a shot
glass to be 'slammed down'.

americano

30 ml Campari
30 ml sweet vermouth
soda water
slice of orange for garnish

Drop some large ice cubes into an old-fashioned glass. Pour in Campari and vermouth, then top with soda. Float the orange slice in the glass and serve with a swizzle stick.

suggested glass: old-fashioned

b52

15 ml Kahlua
15 ml Irish cream
15 ml Cointreau

Carefully pour the ingredients, in the order given, over the back of a spoon, to create a layered effect.

suggested glass: old-fashioned or shot glass

You can use Grand Marnier instead of Cointreau, or just a triple sec if you prefer.

bahama mama

15 ml Malibu
15 ml Kahlua
15 ml dark rum
15 ml white rum
pineapple juice
pineapple wedge and mint
sprig for garnish

Shake Malibu, Kahlua, dark and white rums well with ice. Strain into a tall glass over fresh crushed ice. Top with pineapple juice and garnish with pineapple wedge and sprig of mint.

suggested glass: highball

chocolate sambuca

30 ml crème de cacao
30 ml sambuca

Pour the crème de cacao into a large shot glass, then pour the sambuca slowly in over the back of a spoon to create a layered effect.

suggested glass: shot glass

duchess

60 ml **Pernod**
15 ml **dry vermouth**
15 ml **sweet vermouth**

Shake all ingredients well with ice and strain into a chilled cocktail glass.

suggested glass: cocktail glass

fallen angel

30 ml advocaat
40 ml cherry advocaat
lemonade
fresh cherries for garnish

Swirl together the two advocaats in a highball glass. Add ice cubes, then top with lemonade. Hang a pair of cherries over the rim of the glass and serve with a swizzle stick and straw.

suggested glass: highball

frangelico cream martini

45 ml Frangelico
20 ml Kahlua
45 ml double cream

Shake the Frangelico and Kahlua well with ice. Pour into a chilled martini glass and slowly pour cream on top.

suggested glass: cocktail glass

fruit tingle

30 ml blue curaçao
30 ml melon liqueur
lemonade
dash of grenadine
maraschino cherry
for garnish

Half-fill a wine glass or goblet with crushed ice (or ice cubes). Pour in curaçao slowly over the back of a spoon, then do the same with the melon liqueur to create a layered effect. Top with lemonade and then a dash of grenadine. Garnish with a cherry and serve with short straws.

suggested glass: wine glass

golden dream

20 ml Galliano
20 ml Cointreau
20 ml orange juice
20 ml cream

Shake ingredients well with ice and strain into a cocktail glass.

suggested glass: cocktail glass

grasshopper

30 ml green crème de menthe
30 ml white crème de cacao
30 ml pouring cream
red and green maraschino
cherries for garnish

Shake the liqueurs and cream well with ice. Strain into a chilled cocktail glass. Spear red and green cherries alternately on a toothpick and place across the top of the glass.

suggested glass: cocktail glass

For a Flying Grasshopper, add 30 ml vodka.

japanese slipper

30 ml Midori
30 ml Cointreau
30 ml lemon juice
slice of honeydew melon

Shake liqueurs and juice
well with ice. Strain into
a champagne saucer and
garnish with melon slice.

suggested glass: champagne
saucer

jelly bean

30 ml ouzo
15 ml blue curaçao
15 ml grenadine
lemonade

Pile ice blocks into a highball glass, then add ouzo, curaçao and grenadine. Stir well. Top up with lemonade and serve with a swizzle stick.

suggested glass: highball

lady m.

45 ml Frangelico
45 ml Midori
1 scoop vanilla ice-cream
good-quality grated chocolate
for garnish

Put Frangelico, Midori and ice-cream in a blender with some crushed ice and blend for 20 seconds. Pour into a tall glass and garnish with grated chocolate.

suggested glass: highball or goblet

London fog

30 ml white crème de menthe
30 ml Pernod
1 scoop vanilla ice-cream

Place ingredients with crushed ice in a blender and blend until frothy. Pour into a large chilled wine glass.

suggested glass: wine glass

mimosa

10 ml orange curaçao
30 ml orange juice
75 ml champagne
or sparkling wine

Pour the curaçao and orange juice into a well-chilled champagne flute and top with champagne.

suggested glass: champagne flute

A Mimosa can also be made without the curaçao – still enjoyable, but not quite as special.

moulin rouge

45 ml sloe gin
30 ml sweet vermouth
dash of Angostura bitters

Stir ingredients in a mixing glass with ice, then strain into a chilled cocktail glass.

suggested glass: cocktail glass

negroni

30 ml Campari
30 ml sweet vermouth
30 ml gin
lemon peel for a twist

Shake Campari, vermouth and gin well with ice, then strain into a short glass or a wine glass over ice, cubes and add a twist of lemon.

suggested glass: old-fashioned or wine glass

One story claims that this short, sharp aperitif – a classic on cocktail lists – was named after Count Camillo Negroni who ordered the drink regularly in the 1920s at a bar in Florence.

orgasm

30 ml Cointreau
30 ml Irish cream

Fill a short glass with ice.
Slowly pour in the Cointreau,
then top with Irish cream.

suggested glass: old-fashioned

You can freeze some cream or Irish cream, in a log shape,
slice this into thick rounds and serve as a garnish.
For a Screaming Orgasm, add 30 ml vodka.

peach tart

30 ml peach schnapps
15 ml fresh lime juice

Stir schnapps and lime juice together with ice, then strain into a chilled shot glass.

suggested glass: shot glass

pimm's

90 ml Pimm's No. 1 Cup

soft drink (lemonade, soda water or dry ginger ale)

slices of cucumber peel, orange and lemon for garnish

Tumble plenty of ice into a highball glass. Top with the Pimm's and fill with soft drink. Garnish generously and serve with a swizzle stick and straw.

suggested glass: highball

The base of Pimm's No. 1 is a mix of herbs, spices and gin; it was invented by James Pimm in 1823 and served at his London oyster bar. At one time there was a Pimm's No. 2 Cup (whisky-based) and No. 3 Cup (brandy), but the gin-based version is now the only one readily available.

pink pussy

30 ml Campari
15 ml peach brandy
dash of egg white
bitter-lemon soft drink

Shake the Campari, peach brandy and egg white with ice until frothy. Strain into a cocktail glass with several fresh ice cubes and top with the bitter-lemon soft drink.

suggested glass: cocktail glass

pink squirrel

30 ml white crème de cacao
30 ml Malibu
30 ml cream
dash of grenadine
cherry and grated nutmeg to garnish

Shake the first four ingredients well with ice. Strain into a cocktail glass. Put the cherry on a toothpick and balance on the glass.
Dust the cocktail with nutmeg.

suggested glass: cocktail glass

raspari

6 fresh raspberries
15 ml fresh lime juice
30 ml Campari
30 ml vodka
15 ml sugar syrup
7 ml black raspberry liqueur

Muddle the raspberries and lime juice in a cocktail shaker. Add the Campari, vodka, sugar syrup and ice, and shake. Strain into a short glass with plenty of crushed ice and top with raspberry liqueur.

suggested glass: old-fashioned

ruby shy

30 ml Malibu
30 ml raspberry cordial
lemonade
freshly grated coconut
for garnish

Half-fill a tall glass with ice cubes. Pour in Malibu and raspberry cordial. Top with lemonade and garnish with the coconut.

suggested glass: highball

seduction

15 ml Kahlua
15 ml melon liqueur
15 ml Irish cream

Pour Kahlua into a shot glass. Then, using the back of a spoon, slowly pour in the melon liqueur, and then the Irish cream, to create three distinct layers.

suggested glass: shot glass

silver bullet

15 ml sambuca
15 ml vodka, well chilled

Pour the ingredients into a chilled shot glass.

suggested glass: shot glass

A Silver Bullet is said to be clear, powerful
and never misses its mark.

snowball

45 ml advocaat
90 ml lemonade
strawberry for garnish

Pour advocaat into a large
wine glass, then slowly add
lemonade while stirring. Float
the strawberry in the glass and
serve with straws.

suggested glass: wine glass

splice

30 ml **Cointreau**
30 ml melon liqueur
15 ml **Malibu**
100 ml pineapple juice
60 ml cream
pineapple wedge and melon ball for garnish

Combine Cointreau, melon liqueur, Malibu, juice and cream in a blender with crushed ice and blend well. Pour into a large wine glass or goblet. Spear pineapple wedge and melon ball on a toothpick and place on side of glass. Serve with a long straw, and cocktail umbrella if desired.

suggested glass: wine glass or goblet

tiger tail

60 ml Pernod
½ teaspoon Cointreau
120 ml orange juice
wedge of lime
for garnish

Combine ingredients in a
blender with ice and blend
until smooth. Pour into a large,
chilled wine glass. Garnish with
lime.

suggested glass: wine glass

toblerone

chocolate syrup, to coat glass
15 ml Frangelico
15 ml Kahlua
15 ml Irish cream
30 ml cream
grated chocolate for garnish

Pour some chocolate syrup into a cocktail glass and twirl the glass to partially coat the inside. Shake the liqueurs and cream with ice, then strain into prepared glass. Sprinkle a little grated chocolate on top.

suggested glass: cocktail glass

rum

american flyer

45 ml white rum
7 ml lime juice
pinch sugar
sparkling white wine
slice of lime for garnish

Combine the rum, lime juice and sugar with ice and shake well. Strain into a cocktail glass and top with sparkling wine. Drop lime slice into the glass.

suggested glass: cocktail glass

blue haze

15 ml parfait amour
15 ml dry vermouth
20 ml white rum
5 ml Cointreau

Pour the ingredients slowly, in this order, into a chilled glass. Place in the refrigerator for 5–10 minutes before serving.

suggested glass: cocktail glass

captain's blood

60 ml dark or golden rum
30 ml fresh lime juice
several dashes of Angostura
bitters
slice of lemon for garnish

Shake ingredients with crushed ice and strain into a chilled old-fashioned glass. Make a twisted ring with the lemon and drop into the drink.

suggested glass: old-fashioned

cuba libra

60 ml white rum

juice of 1 lime (keep lime halves for garnish)

cola soft drink

Pour the rum and lime juice into a highball glass, then add the lime halves and some ice and top with cola. Serve with straws.

suggested glass: highball

daiquiri

45 ml white rum
30 ml lime juice
15 ml sugar syrup
long strip of lime peel
for garnish

Shake all ingredients well with ice and strain into a cocktail glass. Tie the lime peel in a knot, drop it into the glass and serve.

suggested glass: cocktail glass

One of the great cocktails, the Daiquiri was created in Havana, reputedly named after a small Cuban town and made famous by Ernest Hemingway. The classic version combines rum with lime juice, but there are endless fruit variations. Leave the sugar out if you prefer a sharper taste, or add a drop of maraschino liqueur for a trace of sweetness.
Some variations follow.

frozen mango daiquiri

45 ml white rum
20 ml lime liqueur
45 ml frozen mango nectar
strawberry for garnish

Blend ingredients with a ice until just blended. Pile into a cocktail glass or champagne saucer and garnish with strawberry.

suggested glass: cocktail glass or champagne saucer

passionfruit daiquiri

45 ml white rum
30 ml lime juice
15 ml passionfruit syrup

Blend ingredients with crushed ice until well blended. Strain into a cocktail glass.

suggested glass: cocktail glass

fluffy duck

30 ml white rum
30 ml advocaat
lemonade
heavy cream
strawberry for garnish

Mix the rum and advocaat in a highball glass with some ice. Pour in lemonade, then float a little cream on top. Cut the strawberry into a fan shape (see page 13) and place on the rim of the glass. Serve with a straw.

suggested glass: highball

gauguin

60 ml white rum
15 ml lemon juice
15 ml lime juice
15 ml passionfruit syrup
maraschino cherry for garnish

Combine the rum, juices and syrup in a blender with cracked ice and blend on low speed until smooth. Pour into a short, chilled glass and garnish with a cherry.

suggested glass: old-fashioned

hurricane

45 ml white rum
45 ml dark rum
30 ml passionfruit syrup
1 tablespoon lime juice
half slice of lime for garnish

Shake liquid ingredients well with cracked ice. Strain into a chilled cocktail glass. Garnish with lime slice on rim of glass and serve with swizzle stick.

suggested glass: cocktail glass

mai tai

juice of 1 lime
30 ml white rum
30 ml dark rum
15 orange curaçao
15 ml amaretto
pineapple spear, lime peel and
fresh mint leaves for garnish

Half-fill a highball glass with ice. Squeeze in the lime juice, then add the rum and liqueurs. Stir with a swizzle stick. Slip the pineapple, lime and mint leaves onto a toothpick and put on the side of the glass. Serve with a straw.

suggested glass: highball

Legend has it that this potent concoction was devised in the 1940s by Victor Bergeron at the original Trader Vic's, an eccentric watering hole in California. When served to some friends from Tahiti they proclaimed it *mai tai* or 'out of this world'.

mojito

fresh mint leaves
15 ml sugar syrup
45 ml lime juice
soda water
60 ml white rum
chunky lime slice and fresh
mint sprigs to garnish

Gently muddle the mint leaves, sugar syrup and lime juice together in a tall glass. Three-quarters fill the glass with crushed ice, then pour in rum and top with soda. Balance the lime wedge on the rim, and add a fresh sprig of mint.

suggested glass: highball

This traditional Cuban cocktail – the name is pronounced
moh-HEE-*toe* – was originally made with sugarcane juice.
If you're feeling celebratory, use champagne or sparkling wine
instead of soda water for a Luxury Mojito.

opal ice

15 ml white rum
15 ml triple sec
10 ml melon liqueur
10 ml blue curaçao
1 tablespoon fresh lime juice

Shake rum, triple sec, melon liqueur and lime juice well with ice. Strain half into a cocktail glass, slowly add the blue curaçao, then top with remaining liquid. Serve with short straws.

suggested glass: cocktail glass

peach tree

60 ml dark rum
60 ml peach syrup
lime wedge for garnish

Fill a short glass with ice cubes, top with rum and peach syrup, and stir. Squeeze in some lime juice and drop in the lime wedge.

suggested glass: old-fashioned

piña colada

60 ml white rum
30 ml coconut cream
120 ml pineapple juice
long spear of pineapple and
maraschino cherry for garnish

Blend liquid ingredients with a scoop of crushed ice, until smooth. Pour into a goblet or highball glass with ice cubes. Put pineapple slice and cherry side-by-side on the rim. Add a cocktail umbrella if you're feeling festive.

suggested glass: goblet or highball

planter's punch

500 ml dark rum
200 ml fresh lime juice
200 ml fresh lemon juice
4 teaspoons castor sugar
1 teaspoon Angostura bitters
500 ml soda water
slices of fresh seasonal fruit
for garnish

Fill punch bowl one-third with ice. Pour in rum, lime and lemon juices, sugar and bitters. Mix together, then top with soda water. Garnish with slices of fresh fruit.

suggested glass: wine glass or highball

This is a drink to share, so this recipe makes enough for 10.
Make sure to keep it well chilled.

rum martini

60 ml light rum
½ teaspoon dry vermouth
dash of orange bitters
slice of orange for garnish

Put rum and vermouth in mixing glass with ice and stir. Strain into chilled cocktail glass and drop orange slice into glass.

suggested glass: cocktail glass

rum runner

15 ml dark rum
15 ml white rum
20 ml crème de banane
20 ml blackberry brandy
15 ml grenadine
20 ml fresh lime juice

Sugar-frost (see page 12) a large chilled, champagne saucer. Shake ingredients together with ice and strain into a prepared glass.

suggested glass: champagne saucer

zombie

45 ml golden rum
20 ml white rum
20 ml dark rum
15 ml each of pineapple, lime and grapefruit juices
1 teaspoon castor sugar
mint leaves and fresh fruit for garnish

Shake all the liquid ingredients and the sugar well with ice. Strain into a highball glass with fresh ice, and garnish with mint leaves and fresh fruit.

suggested glass: highball

A delicious but perilously alcoholic cocktail for those who enjoy rum in any – and every – form.

sake

kabuki

60 ml sake
15 ml Cointreau
15 ml sugar syrup
30 ml lime cordial
lime peel for a twist

Salt-frost a tall glass (see page 12). Pour sake, Cointreau, sugar syrup and cordial into a blender. Blend well and pour into prepared glass. Add twist to the drink before serving.

suggested glass: highball

midnight samurai

30 ml sake
20 ml Kahlua

Shake ingredients with ice and strain into a chilled cocktail glass.

suggested glass: cocktail glass

saketini

30 ml sake
60 ml vodka
dash of dry vermouth
sliver of cucumber peel
for garnish

Half-fill a mixing glass with ice.
Pour in the sake, vodka and
vermouth. Stir well, then strain
into a chilled cocktail glass
and garnish with the
cucumber peel.

suggested glass: cocktail glass

tequila

ambassador

60 ml tequila
30 ml sugar syrup
orange juice
slice of orange for garnish

Pile ice cubes into a glass, then pour in tequila and sugar syrup and top with juice. Mix gently until glass frosts. Balance orange slice on the rim of the glass.

suggested glass: old-fashioned

blood orange margarita

45 ml golden tequila
30 ml blood orange juice
30 ml fresh lime juice
30 ml sugar syrup
slice of blood orange or lime
for garnish

Dip rim of a large cocktail glass into lime juice and then salt-frost (see page 12). Shake ingredients well with ice and strain into the prepared glass. Garnish with orange or lime slice.

suggested glass: cocktail glass

brave bull

45 ml silver tequila
30 ml coffee liqueur
sliver of lemon peel for
garnish

Put some ice cubes into a short, chilled glass. Pour in tequila and coffee liqueur, and stir. Garnish with lemon peel.

suggested glass: old-fashioned

el diablo

60 ml tequila
10 ml crème de cassis
dry ginger ale
lime wedge

Half-fill a tall glass with ice.
Pour in tequila and crème de
cassis, then top with dry ginger.
Squeeze in a little lime juice
and then drop the wedge into
the glass. Stir, then serve.

suggested glass: highball or other
tall glass

lolita

20 ml tequila
10 ml lime juice
1 teaspoon honey
2 dashes of Angostura
bitters

Shake ingredients with ice,
then strain into a chilled
cocktail glass and add an
ice cube or two.

suggested glass: cocktail glass

margarita

45 ml tequila

15 ml Cointreau or triple sec

10 ml fresh lime or lemon juice

Salt-frost the rim of a cocktail glass (see page 12). Shake the ingredients together well then strain into the prepared glass.

suggested glass: cocktail glass

margarita (frozen)

45 ml tequila
15 ml Cointreau or triple sec
30 ml fresh lime juice
lime wedge for garnish

Salt-frost the rim of a cocktail glass (see page 12). Blend tequila, Cointreau, lime juice and crushed ice in a blender until mixture resembles shaved ice. Pour into the prepared glass and garnish with wedge of lime.

suggested glass: cocktail glass

mexicola

60 ml silver tequila
cola soft drink
lime wedge

Put ice cubes into a tall, chilled glass, then pour in tequila and top with cola. Squeeze a few drops of lime juice into the glass, then drop in the wedge.

suggested glass: highball

tequila fresa

45 ml tequila
15 ml strawberry liqueur
10 ml fresh lime juice
dash of orange bitters
slice of lime and a strawberry
for garnish

Shake ingredients well with
ice, then strain into a chilled
cocktail glass. Pierce the lime
slice and strawberry with a
toothpick and place on rim
of glass.

suggested glass: cocktail glass

tequila sunrise

45 ml tequila
100 ml orange juice
10 ml grenadine
½ orange slice for garnish

Put plenty of ice in a tall glass. Top with tequila and orange juice, then pour in grenadine – it will float to the bottom to create a 'sunrise'. Garnish with orange slice and serve with straws.

suggested glass: highball

For a Tequila Sunset, use crème de cassis or blackberry brandy in place of grenadine.

vodka

black russian

30 ml vodka
20 ml Kahlua
cola soft drink
(optional)

Shake vodka and Kahlua well with ice. Strain into a cocktail glass with fresh crushed ice. Add a dash of cola if desired.

suggested glass: cocktail glass

bloody mary

45 ml vodka
90 ml tomato juice
juice of ½ lemon
few dashes each of Tabasco
and Worcestershire sauces
salt and freshly ground
black pepper
slice of lemon and a celery
stalk for garnish

Mix vodka and juices with ice and stir well. Strain into tall chilled glass and add fresh ice. Season with salt and pepper if desired. Float the lemon slice in the glass and serve with a crisp celery stalk to use as a swizzle stick.

suggested glass: highball

For a Virgin Mary, omit the vodka.
A Chilli Mary uses chilli-infused vodka.
A Vampiro uses tequila instead of vodka.

bullshot

45 ml vodka
120 ml beef stock
dash of Worcestershire sauce
dash of Tabasco sauce
(optional)
20 ml lemon juice
salt and freshly ground pepper
lemon slice for garnish

Mix all the ingredients in a mixing glass or jug, with ice. Strain into a tall glass with fresh ice and add the lemon slice.

suggested glass: highball

This is regarded by some as a highly restorative, 'morning after' cocktail.

caipiroska

45 ml vodka
1 lime cut into 8 wedges
2 teaspoons castor sugar

Put the lime wedges and sugar into a cocktail shaker and use a muddler to crush the sugar into the wedges. Add vodka, shake well with ice and then pour into glass.

suggested glass: old-fashioned

chi-chi

45 ml vodka

15 ml Malibu

30 ml coconut cream

125 ml pineapple juice

pineapple wedge and a fresh
flower (optional) for garnish

Combine vodka, Malibu, coconut cream and pineapple juice in a blender with crushed ice and blend well. Pour into a large wine glass or goblet and garnish with pineapple wedge and strawberry.

suggested glass: wine glass or highball

chocolate cake

30 ml vanilla vodka
15 ml Frangelico
15 ml crème de cacao
15 ml Malibu
(or other coconut liqueur)

Put 3–4 ice cubes in a tall glass. Add all ingredients, stir gently and serve.

suggested glass: highball

cordless screwdriver

45 ml vodka, well chilled
orange wedge
castor sugar

Pour the vodka into a shot glass. Dip the orange wedge into sugar. The procedure is to 'slam' the vodka shot, then bite into the orange.

suggested glass: shot glass

For a variation, try mandarin-flavoured vodka instead of plain vodka.

cosmopolitan

60 ml vodka
30 ml Cointreau (or triple sec)
30 ml fresh lime juice
30 ml cranberry juice
lime peel for a twist
lime spiral for garnish

Shake all the liquid ingredients with ice. Strain into a cocktail glass. Add a twist of lime and garnish with a lime spiral.

suggested glass: cocktail glass

espresso martini

45 ml vodka
45 ml Kahlua
30 ml white crème de cacao
30 ml cold espresso coffee
2–3 coffee beans for garnish

Shake liquid ingredients well with ice (you want it quite frothy), then strain into a cocktail glass. Garnish with coffee beans.

suggested glass: cocktail glass

harvey wallbanger

60 ml vodka
20 ml Galliano
100–120 ml orange juice
orange peel for garnish

Put plenty of ice into a highball glass. Pour in vodka and Galliano, and stir to combine. Top with orange juice and garnish with a length of peel tied into a knot.

suggested glass: highball

kamikaze

30 ml vodka
30 ml Cointreau
30 ml lemon juice
5 ml lime cordial
sliver of lime peel for garnish

Shake liquid ingredients well with ice. Strain into a cocktail glass or champagne saucer, then drop in the lime peel.

suggested glass: cocktail glass

For those in a hurry, a Kamikaze Flyer consists just of vodka and Cointreau, served in a shot glass and downed in one shot. It's well named.

lemon drop

45 ml vodka, chilled
lemon wedge
castor sugar

Pour vodka into a shot glass.
Dip lemon wedge in sugar.
Shoot the vodka and then bite
into the lemon wedge and suck
on it.

suggested glass: shot glass

long island iced tea

20 ml vodka
20 ml tequila
20 ml white rum
10 ml Cointreau
20 ml lemon juice
20 ml sugar syrup
dash of cola soft drink
spiral of lemon peel
for garnish

Put some ice cubes in a tall glass. Pour in the spirits and Cointreau, then add lemon juice and sugar syrup. Stir to mix, add a dash of cola and drop the lemon peel into the glass. Sip mighty slowly.

suggested glass: highball

While it's true this concoction bears some resemblance to iced tea, its innocent look disguises a powerful kick. For a change, use dry ginger in place of cola, and lime peel for the garnish.

madras

45 ml vodka
120 ml cranberry juice
30 ml orange juice
lime wedge
berries for garnish

Put ice into a tall glass, then pour in vodka and juices. Add a squeeze of lime juice, thread berries on a toothpick and prop in the glass.

suggested glass: highball

melon ball

30 ml vodka
30 ml melon liqueur
orange juice
cherry for garnish

Put ice cubes in a tall glass, add vodka and melon liqueur, then top with orange juice. Garnish with a cherry and serve with a swizzle stick and straw.

suggested glass: highball

moscow mule

45 ml vodka
20 ml fresh lime juice
ginger beer
long sliver of cucumber peel
and a lime slice for garnish

Pile ice into a highball glass, and add vodka and lime juice. Top up with ginger beer and then stir. Put the cucumber peel in the drink and fix the lime to the edge of the glass. Serve with straws.

suggested glass: highball

pink hound

30 ml vodka
120–150 ml ruby grapefruit
juice
slice of ruby grapefruit
for garnish

Pour the vodka into a tall glass with ice, top with ruby grapefruit juice. Squeeze a dash of lime juice into the glass, then drop in the grapefruit slice.

suggested glass: highball.

russian espresso

45 ml vodka
20 ml espresso coffee liqueur
lemon peel for a twist

Shake vodka and coffee liqueur with ice. Strain into a chilled cocktail glass and add a twist of lemon.

suggested glass: cocktail glass

salty dog

60 ml vodka
grapefruit juice
long sliver of grapefruit peel
for garnish

Use lemon juice to salt-frost the rim of an old-fashioned glass (see page 12). Drop three or four ice cubes into the glass, top with vodka and grapefruit juice. Tie the peel in a knot and drop into the glass.

suggested glass: old-fashioned

screwdriver

45 ml vodka
60 ml orange juice
slice of orange for garnish

Put ice cubes in a short glass, then pour in vodka and orange juice. Cut orange slice in half and put both pieces on the rim of the glass.

suggested glass: old-fashioned

Cocktail folklore attributes this drink's curious name to Americans employed on oil rigs in Iran, who mixed vodka with orange and stirred it with the screwdrivers they carried as part of their working kit. True or not, it's a colourful tale.

seabreeze

30 ml vodka
60 ml cranberry juice
60 ml grapefruit juice
lime peel and/or a slice of ruby
grapefruit for garnish

Pour the vodka and juices
into a tall glass with ice cubes,
and stir. Garnish with peel
and/or a slice of grapefruit.

suggested glass: highball

sex on the beach

45 ml vodka
30 ml peach schnapps
45 ml pineapple juice
45 ml cranberry juice

Shake all ingredients well with ice. Strain into a cocktail glass with fresh crushed ice.

suggested glass: cocktail glass

sorbet vodka shot

**1 small scoop
raspberry sorbet**

1 tablespoon raspberry vodka

Put the sorbet into a shot glass.
Pour the vodka over, then serve.

suggested glass: shot glass

vanilla rose

30 ml vanilla vodka
15 ml rosewater
15 ml sugar syrup
30 ml ruby grapefruit juice
pink rose petals for garnish

Shake liquid ingredients well with ice. Strain into your most elegant, chilled cocktail glass. Float a rose petal in each glass.

suggested glass: cocktail glass

vodka, melon, mint

2–3 fresh mint leaves
30 ml vodka
120 ml fresh watermelon juice
1 teaspoon lime juice

Put mint leaves in a tall glass and bruise with a muddler or bar spoon to release the flavour. Add plenty of ice cubes, then pour in vodka and juices, and stir well.

suggested glass: old-fashioned

This is one of the newer, refreshing, fruity cocktails.
Add 15 ml of Midori melon liqueur for a little extra fruit flavour.

vodkatini

45 ml vodka
20 ml dry vermouth
lemon peel for a twist

Stir the vodka and the vermouth
in a mixing glass with ice, then
strain into a cocktail glass.
Add a twist of lemon.

suggested glass: cocktail glass

This is also known as a Vodka Martini.

white russian

30 ml vodka
30 ml Kahlua
30 ml milk
30 ml pouring cream
maraschino cherry for garnish

Put ice cubes in a glass. Pour in vodka and Kahlua, then add milk and cream. Stir well and garnish with a cherry.

suggested glass: old-fashioned

whiskey

godfather

45 ml Scotch whisky
30 ml amaretto

Put plenty of ice cubes in a glass, then add the whisky and amaretto. Stir and serve.

suggested glass: old-fashioned

horse's neck

60 ml whiskey
3 dashes Angostura bitters
dry ginger ale
spiral of lemon peel
for garnish

Half-fill a tall glass with ice cubes, pour in whiskey and bitters, then top with dry ginger ale. Drape the lemon spiral over the side of the glass.

suggested glass: highball

manhattan

60 ml rye whiskey
(or use bourbon)
30 ml sweet vermouth
maraschino cherry for garnish

Stir in a mixing glass with ice.
Strain into a cocktail glass and
drop in a single cherry.

suggested glass: cocktail glass

Some drinkers like a dash of Angostura bitters in their Manhattan.
A Dry Manhattan uses dry vermouth instead of sweet,
and includes a twist of lemon.
A Perfect Manhattan uses 15 ml each of sweet and dry vermouth.

old-fashioned

sugar cube
dash of Angostura bitters
1 teaspoon water
60 ml whiskey or bourbon
lemon peel for a twist

Put the sugar cube in a glass. Add bitters and water, and muddle to dissolve. Add whiskey and some ice cubes, then stir. Add a twist of lemon to the glass.

suggested glass: old-fashioned

rob roy

30 ml Scotch whisky
30 ml sweet vermouth
dash of Angostura bitters
maraschino cherry for garnish

Stir ingredients in a mixing glass with ice. Strain into a large wine glass, with fresh ice cubes. Drop in a cherry and serve.

suggested glass: wine glass

rusty nail

30 ml Scotch whisky
45 ml Drambuie
lemon peel for twist (optional)

Pour Scotch and Drambuie into a short glass, with ice. Add a twist of lemon.

suggested glass: old-fashioned

whiskey rickey

60 ml whiskey
30 ml fresh lime juice
soda water
slice of lime for garnish

Half-fill a tall glass with ice cubes. Pour in whiskey and lime juice, then top with soda water. Garnish with lime slice.

suggested glass: highball glass

whiskey sour

60 ml bourbon or rye whiskey
20 ml lemon juice
1 teaspoon castor sugar
spiral of lemon peel for garnish (optional)

Shake liquid ingredients with ice, then strain into a chilled cocktail glass. Garnish with lemon peel if desired.

suggested glass: cocktail glass

For a Vodka Sour, substitute vodka for the whiskey.

wine, sparkling wine & champagne

a goodnight kiss

1 sugar cube
1 drop Angostura bitters
125 ml champagne
or sparkling wine
splash of Campari

Place the sugar cube in a chilled champagne flute and sprinkle with bitters. Pour in ice-cold champagne and add a splash of Campari.

suggested glass: champagne flute

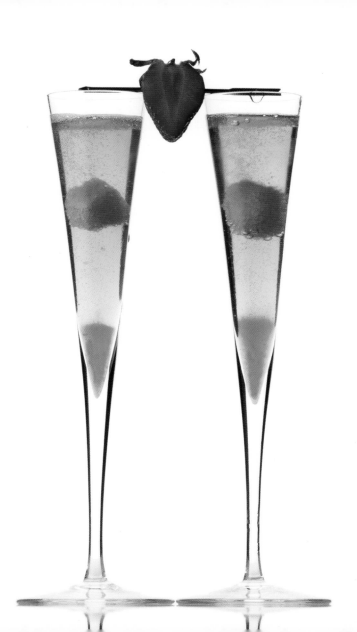

bellini

1 fresh white peach, peeled
a little castor sugar
sparkling white wine
(or champagne,
or Italian prosecco)

Purée the peach with the sugar.
Pour purée into two chilled
glasses, and top slowly with
sparkling wine. Serves 2.

suggested glass: champagne
saucer or cocktail glass

The Bellini is said to have been created at Harry's Bar in Venice,
in honour of Italian Renaissance painter Giovanni Bellini. But then
some say it was invented at the Hotel Danieli . . . whichever is the
case, it's a sophisticated summer aperitif.

black velvet

140 ml English stout
(Guinness is ideal)

140 ml sparkling wine or
champagne

Pour stout and champagne into a jug to mix, then decant into chilled champagne flute.

suggested glass: champagne flute

champagne cocktail

sugar cube
dash of Angostura bitters
15 ml brandy
100 ml champagne
or sparkling wine
a strawberry for garnish

Place the sugar cube in a champagne saucer or flute and sprinkle with bitters. Add brandy, then top with champagne. Garnish with the strawberry.

suggested glass: champagne saucer or flute

death in the afternoon

45 ml Pernod

**125 ml champagne
or sparkling wine**

Pour the Pernod into a chilled
champagne flute and top with
champagne.

suggested glass: champagne flute

This sparkling cocktail was apparently yet another favourite
of Ernest Hemingway and was named after one of his novels.

kir royale

5–10 ml crème de cassis
champagne or sparkling wine

Pour the cassis into your
finest champagne flute
(very well-chilled) and top
with champagne.

suggested glass: champagne flute

An elegant aperitif – the better the champagne,
the better the cocktail. For a simple Kir, add cassis
to a well-chilled dry white wine.

mango bellini

10 ml mango liqueur
30 ml mango nectar
5 ml fresh lime juice
100 ml champagne or
sparkling wine

Put mango liqueur, nectar
and lime juice in a chilled
champagne flute and top
with ice-cold champagne.

suggested glass: champagne flute

For a variation, gently muddle 3 or 4 small fresh basil leaves
with the mango liqueur in the bottom of the glass before adding
the other ingredients.

mocktails
(non-alcoholic)

baby bellini

60 ml peach nectar
30 ml lemon juice
sparkling apple cider

Pour the nectar and juice into
a chilled champagne flute.
Top with cider, and stir.

suggested glass: champagne flute

lychee mint mocktail

3–4 fresh lychees, peeled

60 ml lychee syrup

60 ml mango nectar

20 ml fresh lime juice

7–8 fresh mint leaves, stalks removed

sprig of mint for garnish

Place lychees, syrup, mango nectar, lime juice, mint leaves and ice cubes in a blender and blend until smooth. Pour into a large, well-chilled glass. Garnish with mint sprig.

suggested glass: cocktail glass

pom pom

30 ml fresh lemon juice
½ egg white
5 ml grenadine
lemonade
slice of lemon and
a maraschino cherry
for garnish

Shake lemon juice, egg white
and grenadine well with ice.
Strain into a tall glass, top
with lemonade, and garnish
with lemon slice and cherry.

suggested glass: highball

strawberry apple sparkler

120 g fresh strawberries,
hulled

80 ml apple juice

1 tablespoon castor sugar

soda water

Blend strawberries with apple juice, sugar and ice until thick. Pour into two tall glasses, top with soda water and stir.

suggested glass: highball

glossary

Names with a capital letter (e.g. Bacardi) are proprietary brands.

advocaat A creamy, sweet, egg and brandy liqueur, a rich yellow in colour. There is also a cherry advocaat, which is a rich pink.

amaretto A luscious Italian liqueur with a sweet almond flavour, said to have first been made in Italy in the 1500s.

Angostura bitters *see* bitters.

aperitif Usually refers to a pre-dinner drink such as champagne, sherry or, more commonly, proprietary drinks such as Campari, Dubonnet and Pernod.

apricot brandy This is usually a liqueur of apricot-infused brandy rather than a true brandy distilled from apricots.

armagnac A very fine example of brandy, made in France.

Bacardi A proprietary brand of white rum.

Bénédictine A sweet, brandy-based alcohol made from plants, herbs and fruit peels. It was originally created by Benedictine monks in 1510 in Normandy, France. The inscription DOM on the bottle is derived from the Bénédictine motto 'To God Most Good Most Great'.

bitters A highly concentrated flavouring made from aromatic roots, flowers, fruits and herbs. Angostura is a brand of bitters combining herbs and spices, originally manufactured in Venezuela in 1824 for its medicinal properties. It is the best known of the bitters and creates the pink tinge in 'pink gin'.

blackcurrant liqueur A thick, sweet liqueur of blackcurrants and brandy, also known as crème de cassis.

blend To mix heavy ingredients, (or lots of them) in a blender, rather than in a cocktail shaker.

bourbon An American whiskey, distilled from a minimum 51 per cent corn with some rye and barley, and produced in Bourbon County, USA. Bourbons are robust with more flavour than traditional *whiskies*.

brandy Usually refers to a spirit distilled from grapes, but can also be used to describe any spirit created from fermented and distilled fruit. Brandy can vary widely in taste from fiery to the smooth, silky flavours of the great French brandies such as armagnac and cognac.

build To layer a drink, by pouring the ingredients in slowly over the back of a spoon. The different densities of certain drinks means that some will float on top of others.

cachaça A potent Brazilian spirit made from sugar cane, and the key ingredient in a Caipirinha cocktail.

calvados A fine French apple brandy produced in the Normandy region.

Campari A brand of rich red Italian bitters, usually served as an aperitif.

champagne Sparkling white wine, created using the méthode champenoise to impart the delicate bubbles, and produced only in the Champagne district of France.

Chartreuse An aromatic French liqueur still produced by Carthusian monks in the foothills of the French Alps. More than 130 herbs and spices are infused, macerated and distilled to produce the Yellow and (slightly more alcoholic) Green Chartreuse.

cherry brandy A cherry liqueur, deep-red in colour.

cognac Very fine, aged brandy produced in the Cognac region in southwest France. There are various grades depending on ageing. VSOP on the bottle stands for 'very special old pale'.

Cointreau The best known of the triple-sec liqueurs, Cointreau is clear, sweet and orange-flavoured.

crème (de) . . . A thick, sweet liqueur with one main, (usually fruit), flavour. Examples include crème de banane (banana), crème de fraise (strawberry), crème de menthe (peppermint) and the delicately pink crème de noyaux (almond). Crème de cacao, a rich chocolate liqueur, is also popular.

crème de cassis One of the most widely used of the crème liqueurs, with a blackcurrant flavour.

curaçao An orange-flavoured liqueur, widely used in cocktails and available in clear, orange and blue (the flavour is the same, but the effect of the coloured varieties is more dramatic in cocktails).

Drambuie A liqueur made from Irish malt whiskey and honey. The name is said to mean 'the drink that satisfies' in Gaelic.

Dubonnet A vermouth-style French aperitif, red in colour, with a slight taste of quinine.

Frangelico A sweet, hazelnut-flavoured Italian liqueur.

Galliano A golden, subtly sweet herbal liqueur with unusual anise, lemon and vanilla flavours.

gin Essential for a cocktail bar, gin is a clear, dry spirit distilled from juniper berries and originally formulated in Holland in the mid 1500s.

Grand Marnier A classic, cognac-based, orange-flavoured liqueur from France.

grenadine A sweet, pink, little- or no-alcohol syrup made from pomegranate juice and widely used in cocktails.

Irish cream A rich chocolate-flavoured liqueur of whiskey and cream with a comparatively low alcohol content.

Jägermeister A dark-red, potent herbal liqueur with a root-beer-like flavour, made in Germany. It is usually consumed iced, and often in shots. The name means 'hunt-master'.

Kahlua A creamy, Mexican liqueur with the flavour of coffee and brandy, often mixed with cream, milk or coffee.

kirsch A clear brandy distilled from black cherries.

Malibu A white rum and coconut liqueur, from the Caribbean.

maraschino A colourless, bittersweet cherry liqueur with a subtle almond flavour, distilled from marasca cherries. Traditionally produced in Dalmatia (now Croatia) and Italy. (Maraschino cherries, widely used as a garnish, are no longer soaked in this liqueur.)

Midori A sweet, bright-green, melon-flavoured Japanese liqueur. There are also generic brands of melon liqueur.

muddle To crush fruit, herbs or sugar in the base of the glass or cocktail shaker. Use a muddler (see page 5), or a wooden spoon.

orange bitters A dry, non-alcoholic essence for adding to cocktails.

ouzo A clear, anise-flavoured Greek spirit distilled from a wide range of herbs, berries and grapes, often drunk as an aperitif. When water is added, ouzo turns cloudy.

parfait amour A sweet, scented, violet-coloured liqueur tasting of orange, flowers and cinnamon (some varieties have a more pronounced rose flavour).

Pernod A brand of French aperitif, clear in colour, with an anise flavour.

It is usually diluted with water, which makes it cloudy. Pastis is a generic name for a drink in this style, but with a more liquorice flavour.

Pimm's No 1 Cup A flavoured herbal-based spirit, produced in England. There were originally several versions of this but the gin-based No 1 Cup is now the only one readily available.

pisco A potent, clear or straw-coloured South American spirit distilled from white grapes and widely consumed in Chile and Peru.

prosecco A dry, Italian, lightly sparkling white wine, more delicate than most champagnes.

rum A spirit distilled from sugar cane or molasses, which comes in a variety of styles, strengths and colours (from 'white' – actually colourless – to dark brown).

sake Often referred to as rice wine, this Japanese liquor is made from fermented rice. It is traditionally drunk warm or at room temperature.

sambuca A clear Italian liqueur with a relatively dry anise flavour, made from infused liquorice and elder bush. A coffee-infused version, sambuca negra, is also available.

Scotch A whisky made in Scotland. In most cases it is a blend of grain and malt whiskies. Aged whiskies are especially highly regarded.

sherry A fortified wine, strictly speaking only a true sherry if it is from the Jerez district of Spain. It comes in various styles, from the superfine and dry *fino* to the dark and sweet *oloroso*. It is drunk mainly as an aperitif.

schnapps A strong, colourless spirit traditionally distilled from fruit with no added sugar. Sweetened versions are also available, the range of flavours including peach, pear and watermelon, and even butterscotch.

sloe gin A red liqueur made from sloe berries steeped in gin. It is the traditional 'stirrup cup' consumed before riding to hounds.

Southern Comfort An American liqueur of whiskey flavoured with peaches, a trace of orange, and spices. It has been produced in the Southern states of America since 1874.

stout A dark, malty, English-style fermented beer.

tequila Distilled from juice taken from the heart of the blue agave plant, this fiery spirit is produced in the Tequila region in Mexico. It is famously consumed in shots, but is also a good base in cocktails. Although some varieties have a yellowish colour (golden) the clear or pale version (silver) is most common.

triple sec A clear, orange-flavoured liqueur, similar to a *curaçao*.

twist A small piece of citrus peel collected with a paring knife, which is twisted over the drink to release the intense, fragrant oils from the skin. The peel is sometimes then dropped into the glass for added flavour and aroma.

vermouth A French-style aperitif available in extra dry, bianco (a slightly less-dry variety) and Italian or sweet (which is red in colour and sometimes known as rosso).

vodka A clear grain spirit, highly distilled and originally produced in Russia and Poland. Vodka has become a key ingredient in many modern cocktails, providing a good neutral alcohol base. A range of flavoured vodkas is also now available, including vanilla, citron and raspberry. Vodka is usually stored in the refrigerator or freezer.

whiskey A spirit distilled from grain with barley malt, sugar and yeast, which produces a strong, dry liquor. Ageing can affect the flavour and quality. Scotch is traditionally spelt 'whisky'.

index

PENGUIN BOOKS

Published by the Penguin Group
Penguin Group (Australia)
250 Camberwell Road, Camberwell, Victoria 3124, Australia
(a division of Pearson Australia Group Pty Ltd)

New York   Toronto   London   Dublin   New Delhi   Auckland   Johannesburg

Penguin Books Ltd, Registered Offices: 80 Strand, London, WC2R 0RL, England

First published by Penguin Group (Australia), 2007

10 9 8 7 6 5 4 3 2

Text and photographs copyright Penguin Group (Australia), 2007

Written by Margaret Barca

Cover and text design by Elizabeth Theodosiadis © Penguin Group (Australia)
Photography by Maikka Trupp
Styling by Deborah McLean

Many thanks to those who supplied beautiful props. Special thanks to dedece for the use of their stunning glassware on pp. ii–iii, 2, 6, 10, 24, 27, 32, 38, 47, 50, 56, 59, 81, 87, 97, 103, 106, 115, 126, 132, 135, 138, 141, 147, 153, 156, 162, 168, 172, 175, 178, 189, 192, 198, 201, 207, 210, 214, 217, 220, 240, 243, 246.

Typeset in Grotesque Light by Post Pre-Press Group, Brisbane, Queensland
Scanning and separations by Splitting Image, Clayton, Victoria
Printed in China by 1010 Printing International Ltd

Cataloguing information for this book is available from the National Library of Australia

ISBN: 978 0 14 300586 5

penguin.com.au